D1244485

Dr. Seuss

Jennifer Strand

abdopublishing.com

Published by Abdo Zoom™, PO Box 398166, Minneapolis, Minnesota 55439. Copyright © 2017 by Abdo Consulting Group, Inc. International copyrights reserved in all countries. No part of this book may be reproduced in any form without written permission from the publisher. Abdo Zoom™ is a trademark and logo of Abdo Consulting Group, Inc.

Printed in the United States of America, North Mankato, Minnesota
062016
092016

Cover Photo: William James Warren/Science Faction/Corbis
Interior Photos: William James Warren/Science Faction/Corbis, 1; Al Ravenna/New York World-Telegram and the Sun Newspaper Photograph Collection/Library of Congress, 5, 16; Denis Tangney Jr/iStockphoto, 6–7; The Tichnor Brothers Collection/Boston Public Library, 7; Seth Poppel/Yearbook Library, 8, 9; John Bryson/ The LIFE Images Collection/Getty Images, 11, 12–13, 13; Gene Lester/Getty Images, 14; Julie Clopper/ Shutterstock Images, 15, 18; Anton Ivanov/Shutterstock Images, 17; Bettmann/Corbis, 19

Editor: Emily Temple
Series Designer: Madeline Berger
Art Direction: Dorothy Toth

Publisher's Cataloging-in-Publication Data
Names: Strand, Jennifer, author.
Title: Dr. Seuss / by Jennifer Strand.
Description: Minneapolis, MN : Abdo Zoom, [2017] | Series: Amazing authors |
    Includes bibliographical references and index.
Identifiers: LCCN 2016941357 | ISBN 9781680792140 (lib. bdg.) |
    ISBN 9781680793826 (ebook) | 9781680794717 (Read-to-me ebook)
Subjects: LCSH: Seuss, Dr.--Juvenile literature. | Authors, American--20th
    Century--Biography--Juvenile literature. | Illustrators--United States--
    Biography--Juvenile literature.
Classification: DDC 813/.52 [B]--dc23
LC record available at http://lccn.loc.gov/2016941357

Table of Contents

Introduction

Theodor Geisel wrote and **illustrated** children's books. His **pen name** was Dr. Seuss. His books had fun drawings and **rhymes**.

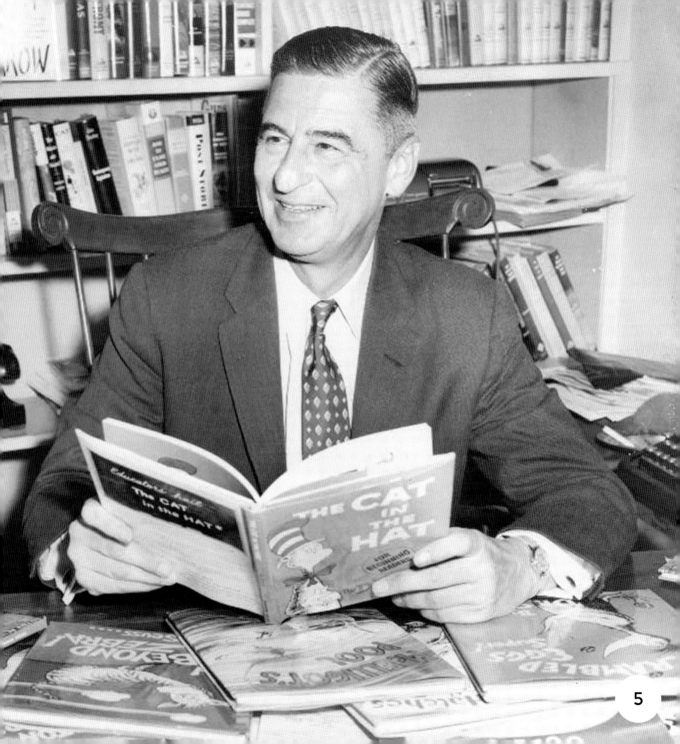

Theodor was born on
March 2, 1904. He lived in
Springfield, Massachusetts.
He was called Ted.

His father worked at a zoo. Ted often went to work with his father.

Ted liked to draw
the animals. But he drew
them in funny shapes.

He also drew cartoons for a school magazine.

Rise to Fame

Later Geisel drew cartoons for magazines and **advertisements**. Then he wrote his first book.

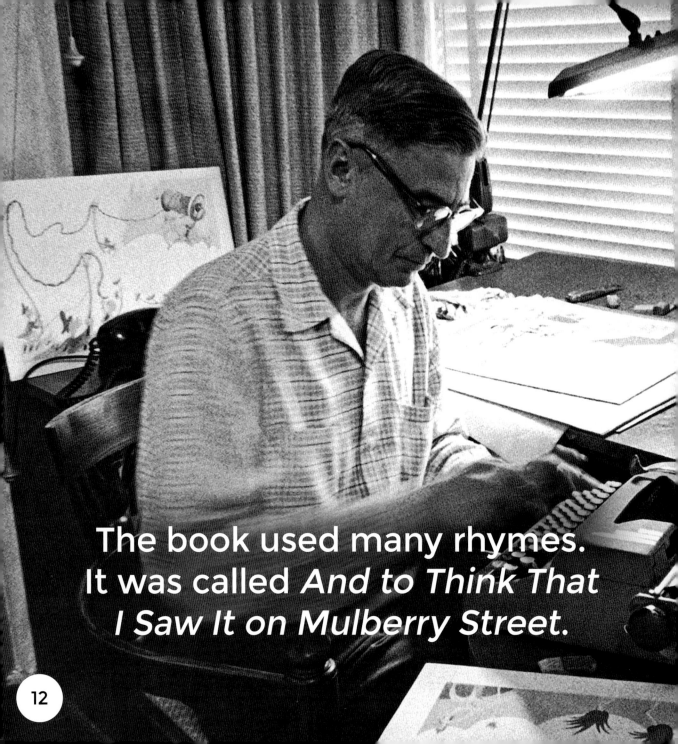

The book used many rhymes. It was called *And to Think That I Saw It on Mulberry Street*.

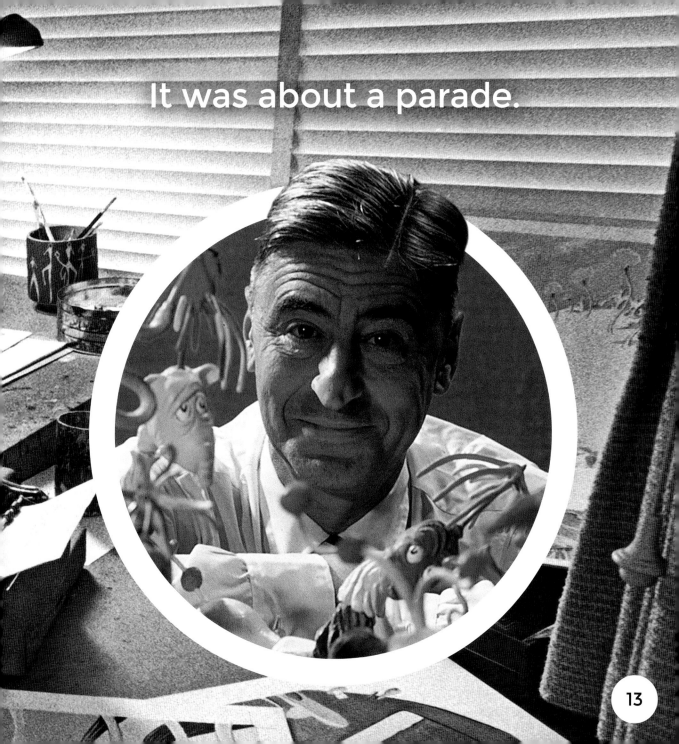

It was about a parade.

13

Geisel wanted to write books that were easier for kids to read.

So he wrote *The Cat in the Hat.* Then he wrote *Green Eggs and Ham.* They became **popular.**

Legacy

Geisel wrote many more books. They had memorable characters.

His favorite was the Grinch from *How the Grinch Stole Christmas.*

His books had fun stories.
They also taught serious lessons.
Some even won awards.

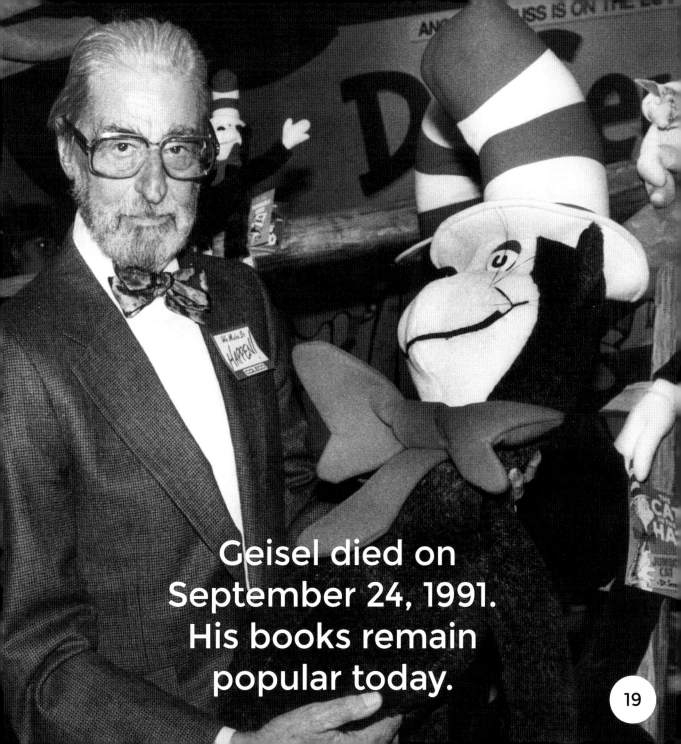

Geisel died on September 24, 1991. His books remain popular today.

Dr. Seuss

Born: March 2, 1904

Birthplace: Springfield, Massachusetts

Known For: Dr. Seuss wrote *The Cat in the Hat* and *Green Eggs and Ham*. His books have fun drawings and rhymes.

Died: September 24, 1991

Key Dates

1904: Theodor Seuss Geisel is born on March 2.

1936: Geisel writes *And to Think That I Saw It on Mulberry Street.*

1957: *The Cat in the Hat* and *How the Grinch Stole Christmas* are published.

1971: Geisel writes *The Lorax.*

1984: Geisel wins the Pulitzer Prize.

1991: Geisel dies on September 24.

Glossary

advertisements - things that help sell products.

characters - people in a story.

illustrated - added pictures to a story.

pen name - a made-up name that an author uses.

popular - liked or enjoyed by many people.

rhymes - when words or phrases end in the same sounds.

Booklinks

For more information
on **Dr. Seuss**, please visit
booklinks.abdopublishing.com

Z In on Biographies!

Learn even more with the Abdo Zoom
Biographies database. Check out
abdozoom.com for more information.

Index